Becoming God's Warrior

A Visual Devotional

To Equip and Empower Women with the Sword of the Spirit

SARAH GOVE

Published by Warrior Women Stand Ministry, LLC
www.warriorwomenstand.com
sgove129@gmail.com
Copyright ©2021 Sarah Gove

Cover design by Rooted Publishing
Cover image from canva.com
Interior photographs by Sarah Gove

ISBN: 978-1-7366882-0-5

Dedicated to all those desiring to
draw closer to Jesus.

Be the Light | Fear Nothing | Combat Evil

Welcome Warrior,

This visual devotional was put together with the desire to help you during times when you feel defeated and discouraged, and to give you resiliency and strength. I pray these devotions bring you encouragement and that they empower you. You have nothing to fear because God is with you. You can move in tandem through the fear because the Holy Spirit is with you. It resides in you through faith in Jesus Christ, who will equip you and God will strengthen you.

Be encouraged through God's Word, the sword of the Spirit. This visual devotional takes you through a Christian journey with Scriptures that will refresh your spirit. It will help you cultivate your warrior woman strength through being the light of Jesus, fearing nothing and combating evil. I pray these pages focus your heart and mind to these three areas as you grow strong in becoming God's warrior. Be equipped and empowered through the strength and comfort that God brings to you, His special warrior woman.

"Put on salvation as your helmet, and take the sword of the Spirit, which is the word of God" (Ephesians 6:17 NLT).

"In the world you will have tribulation; but be of good cheer, I have overcome the world" (John 16:33b).

When you believe that Jesus is your Savior and died for your sins, you invite joy into your soul because death has been defeated. Do not fear things of this world, such as failures, health issues, and societal status because He has already won. During times of tough struggle and situations, you must remember what Jesus has done for you. His overcoming the world can bring you peace and comfort.

St. Paul's Anglican Church, from Sackville Waterfowl Park, New Brunswick, Canada

Burntcoat Head Park, Noel, Nova Scotia, Canada

"Count it all joy when you fall into various trials, knowing that the testing of your faith produces patience. But let patience have its perfect work, that you may be perfect and complete, lacking nothing. If any of you lacks wisdom, let him ask of God" (James 1:2–5).

Joy

Life's challenges can get you down and be more than you think you can bear. But your character will grow in wisdom and understanding as you pass through these trials. God doesn't want to leave you where you are. He wants you to grow and mature. Testing produces character growth. Let it bring joy knowing that God will bring about perfect work in you when you go through struggles.

"And we know that all things work together for good to those who love God, to those who are called according to His purpose" (Romans 8:28).

When something doesn't seem to be going how it "ought" to go, I ask myself, why is this happening? For example, I do not know why I had to go through a miscarriage. But God took me through this tough situation and I have faith that He will use this for His good plan and purpose. Have you ever asked why? You might not know why, but take comfort, God is always faithful in all events and circumstances of your life and cares deeply for you. God, as righteous judge, will make your tough times right in His eyes. God will take everything, even your trials, and produce life-giving good from them. Though you may not understand why you have to go through these life situations, you can have peace knowing that He will use all things for good and His glory.

"But the Lord is faithful, who will establish you and guard you from the evil one" (2 Thessalonians 3:3).

When you are persecuted, you can put your trust in God, who will never let you go. God is in control and will protect you from the evil surrounding you. This brings about confidence to continue with endurance, pressing forward through the hardships and challenges. God will make a way for you. Welcome Jesus into your heart. He will cover you with sheltering wings and set the trajectory before you. He will smile at you, as His child and as you follow His guiding wings, you will soar.

"And He said to me, 'My grace is sufficient for you, for My strength is made perfect in weakness.' Therefore most gladly I will rather boast in my infirmities, that the power of Christ may rest upon me" (2 Corinthians 12:9).

To stand in your own strength is like riding a wobbly bike with no hands; however, if you can rely on God's strength to hold you up, then you have support for standing firm in your weaknesses. He walks with you through your infirmities. Instead of resenting your circumstances, you can see God through your limitations and give God your troubles. God is in control and can handle your limitations and struggles. Your weakness and humanity show God's glory and awesome power. As you accept His grace, you can watch God take the handle bars and lead you through your challenging situations.

Pemaquid Point Lighthouse, Bristol, Maine, USA

"For God has not given us a spirit of fear, but of power and of love, and of a sound mind" (2 Timothy 1:7).

Love

Fear and worry saps your energy and focus to the extent you have nothing left to give. You can shed the spirit of darkness that surrounds you by remembering who is in control. Don't let your Holy Spirit be filled with fear or else there will be no more room for Christ-mindedness. This doesn't mean that you won't have sorrow and feel other emotions, but it means you won't dwell on them because you know who is in control. You can spend your energy fighting using the Word of God.

"Be strong in the Lord and in the power of His might. Put on the whole armor of God, that you may be able to stand against the wiles of the devil" (Ephesians 6:10–11).

The same power that resurrected Jesus from the dead is within you. Through faith you can fight courageously, knowing that you are protected with the whole armor of God. Stand up against the world, the flesh and the devil by defending with truth, righteousness, peace, faithfulness and salvation. Fight back as Jesus taught you, with the sword of the Spirit, which is the Word of God.

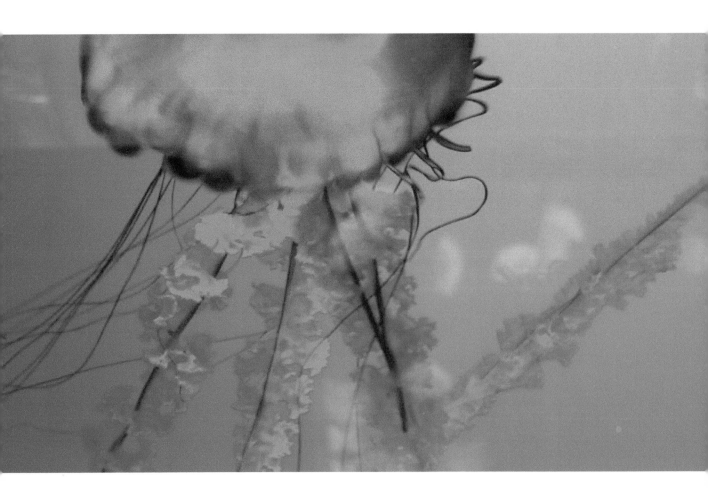

Holy Spirit

"Now may the God of hope fill you with all joy and peace in believing that you may abound in hope by the power of the Holy Spirit" (Romans 15:13).

Hope brings joy and peace during the least expected moments. Even when you are living through heartbreaks and disappointments, hope is knowing joy and peace reigns through God's loving grace. Though you live in a fallen world and bad things happen, you can have hope during these hard times. Because you are a woman warrior of God, He will protect and strengthen you.

Pemaquid Point Lighthouse, Bristol, Maine, USA

"Therefore let us pursue the things which make for peace and the things by which one may edify another" (Romans 14:19).

Let your actions and thoughts assume you don't know the whole story and that others are acting in best intentions. Behave in a way only of support and care for one another. Let your selfishness turn to selflessness. Bring into focus the needs of others and help them as Jesus would want you to. Let God be the judge and He will bring you peace, because God desires for you to love everyone no matter how they have wronged you.

Shenandoah National Park, Skyline Drive, Virginia, USA

"Yea, though I walk through the valley of the shadow of death, I will fear no evil; for You are with me; Your rod and Your staff, they comfort me" (Psalm 23:4).

He will slay your nightmares and direct your travels. Valleys come in all different shapes and sizes. They could be loss of someone dear to you, personal health issues, or an emotional situation. These valleys might be dark, but you are not alone as you are on journey's walk. God has victory over death so there is nothing to fear. His rod protects you and His staff is your guide. Lean upon Him for comfort, support, protection, and counsel.

Montmorency Falls, Quebec City, Quebec, Canada

"When you pass through the waters, I will be with you; and through the rivers, they shall not overflow you. When you walk through the fire, you shall not be burned, nor shall the flame scorch you" (Isaiah 43:2).

God promises that He will protect you against the evil enemy and that you will thrive through the challenges you face in life because of His compassion and love for you. You might face challenges from addictions, unforgiveness or health issues. But remember that God is in control and His loving protection will keep you safe. When you go through struggles, lean on God's strength and you will persevere.

"In God (I will praise His word), In God I have put my trust; I shall not fear. What can flesh do to me?" (Psalm 56:4).

When you are under God's protection, you have nothing to fear. God's protection comes from faith in Jesus Christ that He has died for your sins so you may have a right relationship with God. Therefore, with God fighting for you, what can anyone do to you? You don't have to fear because there is nothing the world can do to take away God's love and protection for you. As you stay near to God, He will stay near to you. He will never drift away.

Cape Breton Highlands National Park, Nova Scotia, Canada

13

"Your word is a lamp to my feet and a light to my path" (Psalm 119:105).

The Bible is God's words and your guide, instructing you how to serve others with love and compassion. Let your actions be as such that they shine God's love and help others see Jesus. God's word lights up the direction you are going. It is your beacon in the night that shows you which way to go. Sometimes the worldly things around you are distracting and you go off God's path, but the Word of God guides you back home.

Emery Path, Acadia National Park, Maine, USA

Bigelow Preserve, Maine, USA

"I lift up my eyes to the mountains – where does my help come from? My help comes from the Lord, the Maker of heaven and earth" (Psalm 121:1–2 NIV).

God, the Creator, has power enough to create everything when He spoke it to be so. In times of need, this same power comes to your aid. Your help comes from the One who has the utmost strength, therefore He can handle anything that comes at you. Draw on God's strength to help emotionally support you when you feel that your life is crumbling around you. When that call comes with unexpected test results informing you of your health status, God will strengthen you. You will find inner strength supporting you.

"For though we walk in the flesh, we do not war according to the flesh. For the weapons of our warfare are not carnal but mighty in God for pulling down strongholds, casting down arguments and every high thing that exalts itself against the knowledge of God, bringing every thought into captivity to the obedience of Christ" (2 Corinthians 10:3–5).

The Bible is your guide in defusing evil and shutting down the enemy, and is your strongest weapon. Scriptures are your weapon to fight the fight in the righteous way, bringing God glory. Defuse evil and shut down the enemy through caring for others and loving those who hate you. Those are actions of a true warrior woman. Jesus never said an eye for an eye; He had compassion and forgave. That is how you are to fight back. The next time someone harms you, reach out and love on them even if you don't think they deserve it. Watch the hate be disarmed.

The Cataracts, North Oxford, Maine, USA

Saguenay Fjords National Park, Rivière-Éternité, Quebec, Canada

"You are the light of the world. A city that is set on a hill cannot be hidden. Nor do they light a lamp and put it under a basket, but on a lampstand, and it gives light to all who are in the house. Let your light so shine before men, that they may see your good works and glorify your Father in heaven" (Matthew 5:14–16).

Do you ever feel that evil is mounting all around you in the world today? When you feel like darkness surrounds you and there seems no way to escape, do this one thing. Be the light. Let your Christlike actions push back the darkness. You can be the change that is needed through righteous living. This revolution will send people wondering what you have that they don't. They will see Christ through you.

"The Lord is on my side; I will not fear" (Psalm 118:6 ESV).

You have nothing to fear because God is your shelter and protection. He will take care of you. What could this world, your flesh, or the enemy bring to you that God can't overcome if it is His will to do so? Nothing can take God's love away from you and that right relationship with your Lord God is all that matters. When all else fades away, love still remains. Therefore, fear nothing. God's got this.

"If God is for us, who can be against us?" (Romans 8:31b).

Jesus claimed victory when He willingly died on the cross and rose again. This makes you right with God. Having God by your side, no one can defeat you because your victory has already been won. You can be confident because of this and continue moving forward through your tough circumstances, like a warrior marching forward into battle with boldness because you know the battle's outcome.

Rumford Whitecap Mountain Preserve, Rumford, Maine, USA

"Be strong and courageous. Do not be afraid or terrified because of them, for the Lord your God goes with you; he will never leave you nor forsake you" (Deuteronomy 31:6 NIV).

Closeness with God comes from a heart's desire to have a right relationship with Him. Draw near to the Father through prayer and Bible reading and He will draw near to you. Feel His closeness and take comfort that you do not have to go it alone. You can trust God because He keeps all His promises. God is with you to help you through tough times and will provide the strength you never thought you had. Hold true to these truths and allow them not only to bring you comfort but to aid you in fighting courageously.

Grand Canyon National Park - South Rim, Arizona, USA

"Fear not, for I am with you; be not dismayed, for I am your God. I will strengthen you" (Isaiah 41:10).

God brings healing and strength to help you through your challenging situations. Trusting God doesn't mean you will not worry; it means you can feel God's strength and it empowers you to continue even when you are anxious. This builds your warrior strength, and your negative feelings slowly lessen because you feel more confident to conquer your tough situations. When you put your trust in God, He will draw near. Think about what tough circumstances you are up against. You have power to work through these because God is with you. Do not be discouraged. Put your trust in the One who is in control instead.

Jordan Pond, Acadia National Park, Maine, USA

"Then Jesus spoke to them again, saying, 'I am the light of the world. He who follows Me shall not walk in darkness, but have the light of life'" (John 8:12).

When you feel that you don't fit in with the choices and decisions others make, you can feel like a fish out of water. Jesus is your light when you feel like you do not belong in this world. Jesus is your hope and your joy for the future. This gives us endurance to continue to push on through the darkness and live for the light.

"And do not be conformed to this world, but be transformed by the renewing of your mind, that you may prove what is that good and acceptable and perfect will of God" (Romans 12:2).

You do not need to be content for what this world has to offer because there is something far greater waiting for you. Sometimes you get so used to the ways of this world that it can become comfortable. Spreading gossip, might not seem so bad, beware of this! Do not be conformed to the sins of this world. Instead, renew your mind. Seek actions that are Christlike. God is so patient and kind. When you make mistakes, He lovingly guides you in character growth. You can look forward to God welcoming you home and saying, "Well done, good and faithful servant" (Matthew 25:23).

Neuschwanstein Castle, Schwangau, Germany

Sainte Anne de Kent, New Brunswick, Canada

"If we live in the Spirit, let us also walk in the Spirit" (Galatians 5:25).

Living and walking in the Spirit means to be in alignment with casting off your sinful ways and letting your actions show your close relationship with Jesus Christ. That can be challenging because you are of flesh and not perfect. Be mindful of your actions and seek to walk in the Spirit. This can be done through continual Bible study and prayer. For example, if you make a mistake, make sure you modify your behavior as the Bible instructs. Jesus is your example of showing compassion and forgiveness. Follow His lead. He loved those who made mistakes, like the woman at the well. She wasn't perfect when she came to the well to fetch water that day, but Jesus showed her love through compassion and forgiveness.

"Be strong and of good courage; do not be afraid, nor be dismayed, for the Lord your God is with you wherever you go" (Joshua 1:9).

Maybe you are battling a health issue like cancer or perhaps you see on the horizon a challenging situation that awaits you. When you look at this road ahead and it seems impossible to conquer, remember that God will be with you through it all. You don't need to look ahead with worry and fear. You might not know how you will get there, yet God will be with you and bring you comfort because you are not alone. God knows what you will experience even before you go through it, and He knows how to support you and guide your actions. This will bring you confidence to boldly step out in faith even though it is scary. Be courageous!

Les Dunes, Tadoussac, Quebec, Canada

"For where your treasure is, there your heart will be also" (Matthew 6:21).

What you choose to spend time and energy on is where your mind and heart are most preoccupied. When you get focused on something, it ends up consuming your time. Then you don't have energy for other things. Building up treasures for heaven and eternity with God instead of the earthly desires and things surrounding you is important to discern. Be encouraged and challenged to seek the wisdom to know the difference between treasures for this world versus treasures for heaven. You cannot serve God and serve things of this world, such as a great wardrobe or popularity.

"The Lord your God, who goes before you, He will fight for you" (Deuteronomy 1:30).

Life can feel defeating when your fingers are worked to the bone and your hard work doesn't seem to be paying off. You might feel like you can never get ahead of all of life's demands and tasks that need your attention. Have you ever felt that the world, the flesh, and the devil seem too hard to fight? It is that feeling of being at your limit and feeling that you cannot go on any further. But remember this: God is out there fighting for you. He is ahead of you on the path called life, conquering your battles.

"Therefore submit to God. Resist the devil and he will flee from you" (James 4:7).

To submit to God means that you willingly put yourself under His authority and control. What better place to be? You cannot control what is around you so why not give it all to the One who can control it all. Instead of caving to human desires, push away from the evil around you and watch the devil scurry off. With God by your side, the enemy will stay away because he fears God. You can rest under God's protection; He has it all under control.

"Search me, O God, and know my heart; try me, and know my anxieties" (Psalm 139:23).

As a warrior, you want God to know your heart and feelings, that He would know and understand what you are going through to support and protect you. Giving your worries to God is easier said than done, but remember that giving your worries to God doesn't mean you don't have emotions. It simply means that you put your trust in God, who is in control of the situation. Don't let your emotions dictate your decisions, let your trust in God do that. Pray to seek God for wisdom and understanding. If you turn your worry list into your prayer list, this soul searching will help you discern where you can grow in God's character.

Aletsch Glacier, Switzerland

"The thief does not come except to steal, and to kill, and to destroy. I have come that they may have life, and that they may have it more abundantly" (John 10:10).

Dangling from the enemy's puppet strings, you can be unknowingly led by him. He wants to use you to steal, kill, and destroy. Be alert for the cunning snake that may try to trick and harm you. He is a liar and ready to deceive when you aren't aware. The devil will flee when you stay connected and in relationship with God through prayer and in His word. Draw near to God, which will cause the thief to depart, and you can live a full life, one that is pure and right in God's eyes.

"To give light to those who sit in darkness and the shadow of death, to guide our feet into the way of peace" (Luke 1:79).

When you see others who are discouraged, give them a helping hand. Show them Jesus' love and help them. Bring them out of the darkness that surrounds them. Be the light for others that they may see God's glory through your Christlike actions. When you spend time helping others, you will find something amazing happen. When you give, it comes back and blesses you too. It brings you joy and happiness when you see others step out of the dark and live in the light.

"But David strengthened himself in the Lord His God" (1 Samuel 30:6b).

When you need strength to work through a tough situation, what do you do first? Call upon your Lord through prayer to guide you instead of trying to make it through the tough situation with your own strength. When David was going through challenging times, he called upon His God and drew strength from God. David gained endurance and wisdom to continue persevering the way God wanted. Draw on God to provide what you need to work through your circumstances and situations. Rely on God's Word to speak truth in your life.

"But the wisdom that is from above is first pure, then peaceable, gentle, willing to yield, full of mercy, and good fruits, without partiality and without hypocrisy" (James 3:17).

Jesus leaves you an example for how to love one another as you would love yourself. Remember He loved His betrayer, Judas. He treated Judas no different than any of the other disciples, for example He washed their feet. The wisdom on how to act dwells in your heart and soul and guides your actions. Pray that your actions and words bring forth pure, peaceable good fruits that make God smile. Desire to leave this world better than you found it.

Rivière Saguenay, Quebec, Canada

Acadia National Park, Maine, USA

"It is God who arms me with strength, and makes my way perfect" (Psalm 18:32).

When you feel weak, God is strong. He will give you the strength you need to walk in the hard times and flourish in His will. What He has planned for you is perfect. When you do not feel properly equipped to do what is needed, realize that God prepares you for what you will experience. You will come out of it with a stronger character.

"Let love be genuine. Abhor what is evil; hold fast to what is good" (Romans 12:9 ESV).

These commands deepen your relationship with Jesus by not only believing that Jesus is your Savior, but that you seek goodness. For example, you can love your neighbors or you can genuinely love your neighbors. To love them genuinely means that your heart wants to reach out to them and help, not because they are deserving but because even in their imperfect state, you care about them. This world seems to showcase so many evil things. Instead, abhor the evil around you. Oppose it and hold tight to what is good. Be like Christ in all you do and how you react to people even when they have wronged you. For example, show others your empathy to their situation without judgment and accusation.

"For I know the thoughts that I think toward you, says the Lord, thoughts of peace and not of evil, to give you a future and a hope" (Jeremiah 29:11).

God wants what is good for you. He has set the plan and is ready to lead and guide. As you decide to follow, the Lord God will bring you to where you could have never imagined. God's plans are beyond your current understanding. And when you take that leap of faith and trust in your good God and follow His lead, amazing things happen.

"But as for you, be strong and courageous, for your work will be rewarded" (2 Chronicles 15:7 NLT).

Be encouraged to do what is right and keep working hard toward the greater eternal goals God has set on your heart. You will find blessings and joy by being obedient to God's plans for you. You can step out in courage and do what God has set out for you.

"But the fruit of the Spirit is love, joy, peace, longsuffering, kindness, goodness, faithfulness, gentleness, self-control" (Galatians 5:22).

Sword of the Spirit

These fruit embody the characteristics of the Holy Spirit living inside you as you walk in the Spirit through faith in Jesus Christ. Jesus gives the Holy Spirit to lead and guide you. As the Holy Spirit offers gentle nudges of conviction, your heart aligns to please the Father. When you turn toward God through prayer and Bible study, you can better discern how the Holy Spirit directs.

"Yet in all these things we are more than conquerors through Him who loved us" (Romans 8:37).

God's love for you was so great that He sent His Son to die for your sins. Jesus claimed victory over death because God's resurrection power conquered all. You can put your faith and trust in Him who loved you first. From His abiding love, you can spread love to others.

Lower Five Islands, Nova Scotia, Canada

"Come to me, all you who are weary and burdened, and I will give you rest" (Matthew 11:28 NIV).

You might struggle with faith in Jesus when there is so much bad in the world. However, Jesus beckons you to come and draw near for He is not of this world. He wants you to trust is in His loving, saving grace. You feel rest because of your faith in the Messiah as your Savior. This brings ultimate peace with God. An earthly peace provides rest, but an eternal peace gives ultimate rest as you bring your burdens before the Lord and lay them down at His feet.

"Trust in the Lord with all your heart, and lean not on your own understanding; in all your ways acknowledge Him, and He shall direct your paths" (Proverbs 3:5–6).

Sometimes you might think your way is best, and it distracts you from the Lord's desire for you. Be aware when this happens and switch to refocus on God. Stay close to God through prayer, bible study and worship to keep your heart, mind, and soul properly focused. This will result in Christlike actions that follow God's will, which in turn results in joy. Trust that His ways and understanding are all encompassing and far exceed your own, then follow His lead.

Bay of Fundy, Nova Scotia, Canada

Five Islands Provincial Park, Five Islands, Nova Scotia, Canada

"Let no corrupt word proceed out of your mouth, but what is good for necessary edification, that it may impart grace to the hearers" (Ephesians 4:29).

Have you ever had that open mouth insert foot situation? You instantly regret what you said and feel horrible for the quick thoughtless response. It is better to use your words to lift others up. It is amazing how powerful your words can impact others through their struggles with support and care. Others will see Jesus in you by your kindness and your words that dispel evil and empower others.

"I will instruct you and teach you in the way you should go; I will guide you with My eye" (Psalm 32:8).

God is like your GPS, directing your actions for a greater purpose than you could ever know. His plans for you are far greater than your own plans. As you are obedient to the calling, He will lead you where He wants you to go. As you let God be your GPS and grab the wheel, listening to Him as He directs you down the path. This leap of faith will amaze. Though you may be heading toward destination unknown, it is fully known to your Guide.

Step Falls Preserve, Newry, Maine, USA

Moncton, New Brunswick, Canada

"You are of God, little children, and have overcome them, because He who is in you is greater than he who is in the world" (1 John 4:4).

Jesus conquered death and the enemy when He sinlessly and willingly died on the cross for your sins. And whoever believes in Jesus has overcome this world too. We are made right with God and can have a relationship with Almighty God. This special relationship brings love, support, and closeness. Eternity awaits! Nothing can separate you from your Conqueror because He washed you white as snow.

"Therefore let us cast off the works of darkness, and let us put on the armor of light" (Romans 13:12).

Believing that Jesus died on the cross to save you from your sins allows you to exit the sin's darkness and enter the light of eternity. Put on your armor to protect yourself and fight against the enemy of darkness. As you shake off those burdens of darkness and grab your warrior armor, your actions are honorable, pure, and good. And your enemies will fall.

Marshall Point Lighthouse, Port Clyde, Maine, USA

"Stay alert! Watch out for your great enemy, the devil. He prowls around like a roaring lion, looking for someone to devour" (1 Peter 5:8 NLT).

When you are following God's will, the enemy wants to deter you. But through prayer God will give you wisdom and understanding, which will help you identify when the enemy is whispering lies in your ear. Pay attention to his sneaky moves and run from the lion's mouth and into the arms of your Protector.

"Therefore we do not lose heart. Even though our outward man is perishing, yet the inward man is being renewed day by day. For our light affliction, which is but for a moment, is working for us a far more exceeding and eternal weight of glory, while we do not look at the things which are seen, but at the things which are not seen. For the things which are seen are temporary, but the things which are not seen are eternal" (2 Corinthians 4:16–18).

The challenges of this life simply do not compare to the amazing joy that will be yours when you are in heaven. Though this earthly life offers much, living for something greater calls for a sacrificial lifestyle. This means leaning toward God's will and being used as a faithful warrior to serve God and others until He calls you home.

Step Falls Preserve, Newry, Maine, USA

Grand Canyon National Park - South Rim, Arizona, USA

"But those who wait on the Lord shall renew their strength; they shall mount up with wings like eagles, they shall run and not be weary, they shall walk and not faint" (Isaiah 40:31).

Sometimes God's will for you is to wait, being prayerful and open to hearing His voice. Then when you receive an answer, be ready to soar. The places God will take you and the things you will do will amaze you. He promises to strengthen and support you. Run with endurance because you are fueled by God's strength, ready to make a godly influence in all that you do.

Alps, Switzerland

"For the word of God is living and powerful, and sharper than any two-edged sword, piercing even to the division of soul and spirit..." (Hebrews 4:12).

Word of God

The truths in the Word of God gently exposes the sin that is deep in our hearts. This identification can bring about a desire to renew your heart and become more Christlike. Studying and knowing the Word of God helps you apply its truths when you are faced with dilemmas. For example, if you had to choose how to respond to an accusing neighbor, you can lean on the Bible's teachings to help guide your actions.

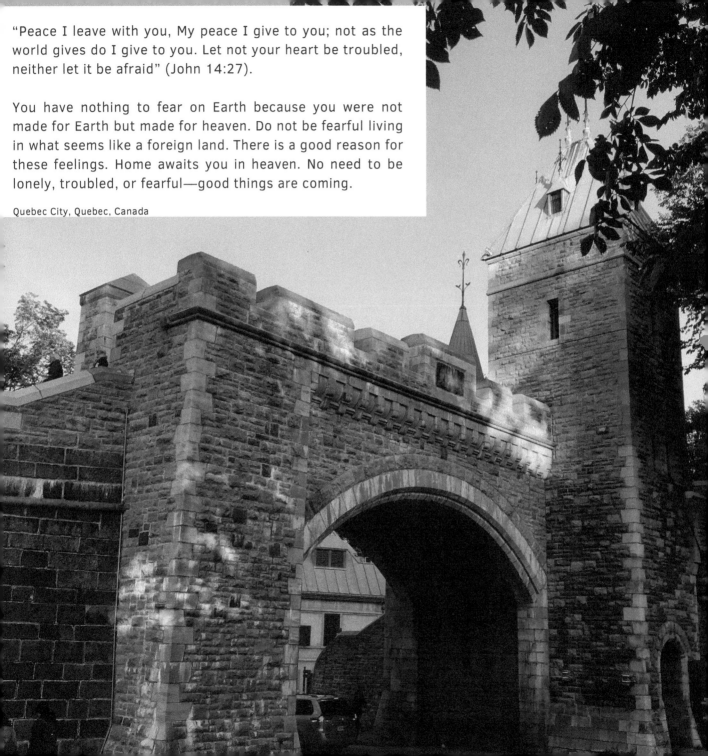

"Peace I leave with you, My peace I give to you; not as the world gives do I give to you. Let not your heart be troubled, neither let it be afraid" (John 14:27).

You have nothing to fear on Earth because you were not made for Earth but made for heaven. Do not be fearful living in what seems like a foreign land. There is a good reason for these feelings. Home awaits you in heaven. No need to be lonely, troubled, or fearful—good things are coming.

Quebec City, Quebec, Canada

"Therefore we also, since we are surrounded by so great a cloud of witnesses, let us lay aside every weight, and the sin which so easily ensnares us, and let us run with endurance the race that is set before us, looking unto Jesus, the author and finisher of our faith, who for the joy that was set before Him endured the cross, despising the shame, and has sat down at the right hand of the throne of God" (Hebrews 12:1–2).

Jesus endured the cross for you and is with you. As you keep your eyes on Jesus and away from your sinful actions, cast aside the sins weighing you down. Allow yourself to be vulnerable before the Lord by humbling your imperfect nature. God wants you as you are. Let this renew your heart, mind, and soul. Now you can live the life God intended for you. Have endurance throughout your life and don't go it alone. Be equipped and run the race through grace and faith.

Northumberland Strait, Canada

"Be anxious for nothing, but in everything by prayer and supplication, with thanksgiving, let your requests be made known to God; and the peace of God, which surpasses all understanding, will guard your hearts and minds through Christ Jesus" (Philippians 4:6–7).

Call upon God and seek His understanding and support. In prayer, anxiousness and fear are brought to rest. You can have peace with God through faith in Jesus. Allow God to take control of your life and watch what He does. As you become a stronger warrior of God, He transforms your understanding. You will see the greater picture of how He goes beyond what you even though possible.

Wood Island Lighthouse, Biddeford, Maine, USA

"Cast your burden on the Lord, and He shall sustain you; He shall never permit the righteous to be moved" (Psalm 55:22).

God wants you to bring Him your tough stuff. He promises to carry your burdens. When you feel you are at the end of your rope and have nothing more to give, God heaps on the strength for you to continue. God desires for you to give Him what you cannot carry. He will lighten your load. You can endure and withstand struggles because God is with you and fights for you.

Mt. Katahdin, Baxter State Park, Maine, USA

"Therefore, if anyone is in Christ, he is a new creation; old things have passed away; behold, all things have become new" (2 Corinthians 5:17).

When you cast aside your old ways and take up your new ways through faith in Jesus Christ, your sins are forgiven. You become a new person in Christ. You are saved and stand in a right relationship with God where you can have peace.

"Finally, brethren, whatever things are true, whatever things are noble, whatever things are just, whatever things are pure, whatever things are lovely, whatever things are of good report, if there is any virtue and if there is anything praiseworthy—meditate on these things (Philippians 4:8).

While spending time on Earth, it is important to live in a Christlike manner that cares for others and glorifies God. Dive into God's Word and learn to practice the disciplines of holiness. Seek to be the light for others to see Jesus and God's glory through your actions. The more you learn from the Bible, the more you make decisions based on this knowledge. Others will see your actions as you lead by this Christlike example and be influenced by it.

Confederation Bridge, New Brunswick - Prince Edward Island, Canada

"Then Jesus said to them, 'A little while longer the light is with you. Walk while you have the light, lest darkness overtake you; he who walks in darkness does not know where he is going'" (John 12:35).

Jesus left you His example, which you are to replicate, and calls you to love everyone as you would love yourself. This is what is meant by being the light for others. When others see the light, it pulls them out of the darkness they are lost in. Help others find Jesus through your example and bring them to the light. This could be as simple as surprising someone with flowers when they are having a tough day.

"But as for you, you meant evil against me; but God meant it for good, in order to bring it about as it is this day, to save many people alive" (Genesis 50:20).

Joseph said these words to his brothers when he forgave them for their poor treatment toward him because Joseph knew that God had greater plans. Life can throw you some things that you do not even know how to get beyond, but God will use all things for His good plans. God will bring about a larger good than you could have even imagined. You might not get to see it all or understand it all, but you must have faith that God's plans are good. Someone else might lie to you or the enemy might attack through gossip, but know that God will use it and bring about a greater good, just like He did for Joseph. Joseph was sold into slavery by his brothers, which God used to save a whole nation from slavery.

"Beloved, do not avenge yourselves, but rather give place to wrath; for it is written, 'Vengeance is Mine, I will repay,' says the Lord" (Romans 12:19).

God is the Righteous Judge. You cannot possibly know everything to judge fairly. You see only one side of a sphere, where God can see all sides and from all angles. You must leave judging up to God, who knows the whole situation. All you have to do is forgive and free yourself from the weight of unforgiveness. You can release yourself from the burden that weighs you down when others hurt your feelings through their selfish actions. Hand it over to God; He will handle the situation.

"Do not be overcome by evil, but overcome evil with good" (Romans 12:21).

Do not give in or let evil take over your actions. Instead, defuse evil by doing good. Take a stand in loving those who have wronged you. Show compassion and forgiveness toward them. Love those who do not deserve it and overtake evil with love.

"And just as you want men to do to you, you also do to them likewise" (Luke 6:31).

When my grandmother would say, "Kill 'em with kindness," I believe she was referring to this verse. You are to treat people how you want to be treated. It does not matter what is done to you. You still need to do to others as you would want people to do to you. You might be shocked by the amazing things that follow. To be nice, I have learned, at times is to be slow to respond. Being kind sets the tone for proper boundaries that produce good responses in others.

"So then, my beloved brethren, let every man be swift to hear, slow to speak, slow to wrath; for the wrath of man does not produce the righteousness of God" (James 1:19–20).

Sometimes jumping too quick with your response will cause regrets. Your words need to produce goodness and not breed hatred. Learning to be slow to respond will help. When a situation occurs that makes you feel things aren't fair, before you respond, pause and pray. This delay in responding allows for time to calm your emotions, think rationally, and respond more appropriately. You can say politely that you will get back to them or simply walk away for the moment. Don't let their wrath bring wrath in you. Instead respond to defuse their wrath.

Prince Edward Island National Park, PEI, Canada

"Hatred stirs up strife, but love covers all sins" (Proverbs 10:12).

Love defuses hate. Try it. Love on someone who, in your opinion, does not deserve it and watch the hatred dissipate and peace show up. Have compassion and empathy for the other person by putting yourself into their situation and seeing how they feel. Think about what might help you in the situation and come along the person in that way. Bring about goodness through your actions toward someone else.

"The light shines in the darkness, and the darkness has not overcome it" (John 1:5 ESV).

Jesus is the light in the darkness. He has victory over it. Rest in knowing that through faith in Jesus, you have victory as well. Darkness cannot overtake the light. Darkness will not win over you because victory is already claimed by the light. Practice your warrior moves by claiming the light and diffusing the evil around you. Show others the love of Jesus through your actions toward them.

Prince Edward Island, Canada

About the Author

Sarah Gove is the founder of Warrior Women Stand Ministry, LLC. A ministry with Jesus Christ as the cornerstone and a focus on becoming godly warrior women, whose heart, mind and soul are set on Christ in all we do and say. Sarah is also the Virtual Director of Ebb & Flow Speaking and Writing. She serves God from a small town in Maine with her amazing family.

🌐 warriorwomenstand.com

f @warriorwomenstand

📷 @warriorwomenstand

✉ sgove129@gmail.com

Visit the website for your free 30 Day Visual Devotional

CPSIA information can be obtained
at www.ICGtesting.com
Printed in the USA
LVHW072207071021
699886LV00002B/45